BUFFALO

THE AMERICAN BISON TODAY

by
DOROTHY HINSHAW PATENT

Photographs by
WILLIAM MUÑOZ

CLARION BOOKS
TICKNOR & FIELDS: A HOUGHTON MIFFLIN COMPANY
NEW YORK

To all those dedicated to preserving the bison,
with special thanks to Ed Merritt

ACKNOWLEDGMENTS

The author and photographer wish to thank Yellowstone
National Park, the National Bison Range at Moiese, Montana,
and Custer State Park, South Dakota, for offering the
opportunities to observe and photograph bison. Special
appreciation goes to Ed Merritt, Jon Malcolm, and Bernard
Hakes for the help they gave during the project.

Clarion Books
Ticknor & Fields, a Houghton Mifflin Company
Text copyright © 1986 by Dorothy Hinshaw Patent
Photographs copyright © 1986 by William Muñoz
All rights reserved. Printed in the U.S.A.

v   10   9   8   7   6   5   4   3   2   1

Library of Congress Cataloging-in-Publication Data
Patent, Dorothy Hinshaw.
    Buffalo: the American bison today.
    Includes index.
    Summary: Describes the life of American bison today
on the National Bison Range in Montana and in other
parks and preserves, with an emphasis on how humans
must carefully manage each herd for its own good.
    1. Bison, American—Juvenile literature. 2. Wild-
life management—Juvenile literature. [1. Bison.
2. Wildlife management] I. Muñoz, William, ill.
II. Title.
QL737.U53P35   1986   333.95'9   85-25483
ISBN 0-89919-345-5

CONTENTS

RULERS OF THE PRAIRIE

The ground shakes as the dark, shaggy animals thunder down the slope toward the roundup pens. Ten to twenty at a time, the animals are chased through the sturdy gate by determined, hollering cowboys. Roundup time has come, as it does every October at the National Bison Range in Montana.

The American Bison, commonly referred to as "buffalo," once roamed the plains of the United States and Canada in countless millions. Now bison live in scattered parks, preserves, and ranches in both countries, their numbers totaling less than 100,000. Wherever they live, they must adapt to the wants and needs of people. Today people must manage the number of bison for the animals' own welfare. Gone are the days when nature just took its course and the bison ruled the prairies.

The bison at the National Bison Range are driven through the gate.

It is hard for us today to imagine the feelings of early white explorers when they encountered the gigantic herds of wandering bison. They could hear the animals coming from miles away. At first the sound was dull, like distant thunder. As the bison got closer, the rumble was transformed into the distinct sound of tramping hooves mingled with the moaning of thousands of animal voices. Then the explorers could see a dark brown tide of bodies coming over a rise. The herds were so big that no one could count the bison. One herd might be

twenty miles wide and over fifty miles long and take days to pass by. "I don't know what to compare them with, except fish in the sea," wrote one early explorer. Some explorers thought there were hundreds of thousands of animals in one herd, others believed there were millions. Altogether, there were thirty to sixty million bison in North America when the white explorers arrived in the 1700s.

For hundreds of years before the coming of the white hunters, the Indians of the plains had depended on the buffalo. To hunt them, they surrounded them on foot, drove them into hidden corrals, or stampeded them over cliffs. They killed them with arrows and spears. The Indians used not only the meat but the skin, horns, bones, hooves, tail, and tendons to make clothing, utensils, weapons, and religious objects. The buffalo were central to the lives of the Plains Indians. To assure a steady supply of meat, many tribes followed the animals as the herds drifted across the prairie.

When white people came bringing horses, the Plains Indians quickly learned to ride and were able to hunt buffalo more effectively. The white explorers, too, went after the buffalo. They slaughtered them by the thousands for their hides and tongues, but they left the rest of the animal to rot on the prairie. By the middle of the nineteenth century, up to a quar-

Indians once stampeded bison over this cliff at the Madison Buffalo Jump State Monument in Montana.

ter-million buffalo skins were harvested each year. Things got even worse in the last quarter of the century, when the transcontinental railroad brought reliable transportation and more people to the plains.

Because of the excesses of the white hunters, the bison, despite their impressive numbers, almost went the way of the once-abundant passenger pigeon, which became extinct in 1914. In the early 1700s, bison lived from southern New York State to southeastern Virginia and Georgia and were common in Pennsylvania and the Ohio Valley. By 1832, there were no buffalo east of the Mississippi River. And by 1900, only twenty wild bison were left in the United States, living in the backcountry of Yellowstone National Park. Only about 250 survived in Canada. A few hundred also remained in private herds. During the late 1800s and early 1900s, bison were protected from hunting. Several herds were established on public lands. Thanks to the efforts of conservationists and private breeders, buffalo live today in parks, preserves, and on ranches throughout the United States and Canada. The American bison has a secure future.

Why does this animal have two names, *bison* and *buffalo*? *Buffalo* is the popular name, given by early white settlers. But the bison is not closely related to other animals called *buffalo*, such as the African buffalo and the Asian water buffalo. Its closest relative is the European bison, or wisent, whose scientific name is *Bison bonasus*. The American bison is named *Bison bison*.

This map at the National Bison Range dramatizes how the territory originally ruled by the buffalo (dark outer line) shrank once the hunters began to use rifles similar to the one displayed.

There are two varieties of American bison, the plains bison and the wood bison. Most buffalo in the United States are pure plains bison, but the Yellowstone herd is mixed. In Canada, the wood buffalo survives in Wood Buffalo National Park in the Northwest Territories, although even there they have bred with plains bison. Only a small number of truly pure wood bison remain. The main difference between the two types is size and color—wood bison are bigger and darker in color than the plains variety.

Bison belong to the same scientific family as the domesticated cow and true buffalo. All these animals have hollow, permanent horns and hooves with two toes each. They are

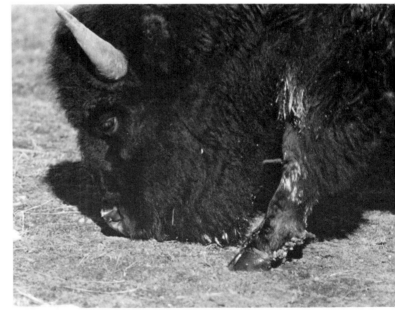

Opposite: Yellowstone National Park, famous for hot springs that cause clouds of steam to rise from the ground, features bison that are a mixture of plains and wood buffalo.

Right: This bison bull is using his tongue to help collect sparse winter feed. Note two toes on his hoof and the permanent horn.

A *bison bull.*

ruminants, which means they have very large, complex stomachs designed to break down the hard-to-digest grass they eat. Ruminants swallow their food and later bring it back into the mouth as a mass called a cud, which the animal chews. After chewing, the cud is swallowed again and the food is digested further.

Although the vast herds that dominated the prairies were awesome, even one lone bison bull is an impressive sight. He is perhaps six feet tall at the shoulder and often weighs in at over a ton. The rear part of his huge body is covered by a sleek coat of chocolate brown. A lighter brown overcoat tops the front of his body, accenting the huge shoulder hump and forming long-haired pantaloons that extend down his forelegs to within

A cow standing in front of a bull.

a foot of the ground. Darker, thick fur grows over his strong, short neck and his massive head, which is decorated by a neat beard and a pair of curved, sharp horns. The fur on his face is especially thick and woolly and can be four to five inches deep between his eyes.

The bison cow is smaller and less massive than the bull, with a thinner neck and smaller hump. She usually weighs around 1,000 pounds, half the weight of a bull. Her horns are smaller than those of the male, and the hair on her head and face is less dense than his. Young cows and bulls have beards of similar lengths. But the cow's beard stops growing when she is a couple of years old, while the bull's continues to get longer and thicker.

Bison do not look streamlined, but they can wheel about in an instant on their slim hind legs and can run as fast as a horse. They can climb rocky slopes and swim deep rivers. Their skinny tails with a tuft at the end are almost constantly in motion. This tail-swishing helps ward off a variety of pesky insects. Bison's sense of smell is well developed, and they can smell water or enemies as far as three miles away. Their eyes are adapted for picking up movement especially well, even a mile away, but they may not notice a nearby object that is completely still. Their ears are able to hear weak and distant sounds.

The tail of this bison looks blurry because it is swishing away flies.

You can see bison of both sexes and various ages

The American buffalo is a social animal, living in groups that vary from as few as a dozen to as many as 200 animals. The gigantic herds of the past were composed of these smaller groups. Cows, calves, and young bulls always stay together. When a herd moves to water or new pasture, mature cows lead

in this herd at Custer State Park in South Dakota.

the way. Although they sometimes join the cows and calves, the mature bulls usually stay together loosely in groups or go off by themselves. But during the breeding season, bulls spend most of their time in the cow herds, where they battle for possession of the females.

WINTER

The bison is superbly adapted to life on the harsh plains. There, winter temperatures can drop past forty degrees below zero, and the wind can whip through the snow drifts for days. As winter approaches, the bison grow a longer, thicker coat to protect them from the frigid days to come. The hair on the back part of the body becomes almost as long as that on the front in the cows and calves.

Many animals have difficulty moving through heavy drifts, but bison are natural snowplows. Using the strong muscles of its hump and neck, a bison can push several feet of snow out of the way to reveal the grass underneath. Other animals are helped by the bison, too, for they can walk along the paths cleared as the buffalo feed.

A bull pushes away the snow so he can feed.

Bison perform another important service to other animals during the winter. Despite their stamina and their heavy coats, some bison do succumb to the harsh conditions, especially old and sick ones. When a bison dies, its body supplies vital food to animals like coyotes and ravens. During the spring, the carcasses of winter-killed bison provide nourishment for grizzly bears when they come out of hibernation.

In the old days, bison would sometimes move in winter a few hundred miles southward, to lower elevations. Or they went into more protected environments where there were trees to break the force of the wind. People used to think that the bison migrated long-distances in the fall and spring, but now we know that is not true. The Yellowstone bison, the only wild herd remaining in the United States, travel to low valleys in the fall and to higher ground in the springtime. These wanderings can cause trouble because the Yellowstone herd is not fenced in and its numbers are not controlled by humans. As the population has grown to over 2,000 animals, bison have begun to leave the park in search of food during the winter months, and nearby ranchers are worried.

The meat of this dead bison nourished coyotes and ravens during the lean times of winter in Yellowstone Park.

Bison can carry a serious cattle disease called brucellosis. Brucellosis is dangerous because it causes a cow to abort her first calf after catching the disease. After that, she can bear young successfully, but both she and her offspring carry the disease. Brucellosis is dangerous to people, too, for it can result in a potentially fatal human disease, undulant fever. Cattle ranches adjoin the north side of Yellowstone, where the park borders on Montana. The bison have learned that there is food outside the park, so they have been leaving in larger and larger numbers to find it. Regular barbed-wire fences are nothing to bison, so they can enter any ranch land at will. But ranchers do not want to risk having their cattle catch brucellosis.

Many suggestions have been made about how to handle the Yellowstone bison in winter. A six-mile-long bison-proof fence could be built where the animals tend to cross out of the park. The bottom wire could be two feet from the ground so that deer, pronghorn, and small animals could pass under it. But such a fence would be very expensive and unattractive. It would also create an unnatural concentration of bison along the park border. The bison would try to leave but could not, and too many might stay.

Bison in Yellowstone Park.

Hunters could be allowed to shoot animals that stray over the boundary. But it would hardly be a real hunt, for the bison do not fear people and are likely just to stand there and be shot. The Montana legislature has passed a bill allowing bison hunts. It remains to be seen whether this will improve the situation.

The Yellowstone bison are not afraid of people. Here, they pay no attention to a snowcat bringing in visiting cross-country skiers.

A Yellowstone bison rests in a winter landscape as steam rises from the hot springs.

While the bison are in the park, they are the responsibility of the National Park Service. But as soon as the Yellowstone bison wander into Montana, they are under the rules of the Montana State Department of Fish, Wildlife, and Parks. This split in responsibility for the management of the big animals only adds to the problem. In 1985, Montana fish and game officials shot bison that left the park and came too near cattle. The meat, heads, and hides of the bison were auctioned off to the highest bidders. As long as the Yellowstone herd is allowed to grow, hungry bison leaving the park during the winter will be a continuing problem.

SPRING & EARLY SUMMER

As the strengthening sun warms the air and melts the snow, the bison begin to shed their long winter coats. They rub their bodies against any object they can find—fenceposts, trees, big rocks. Large stones may be polished to a shine by the activities of the shedding animals. Trees may have their bark rubbed off six feet from the ground. In the early days of the white settlers, telegraph poles were often downed by rubbing bison, and at least one settler lost his entire cabin to itchy buffalo. Their hair comes off in patches, and the animals look very mangy for several months, on into early summer.

A calf and its mother graze together.
Notice the shedding winter coat of the cow.

Bison calves are born in the late spring, starting in April; most enter the world in early May. Twins are very rare among bison. The mother usually moves a short distance away from the herd when it is time to give birth. Her calf is born a few yards from where the other cows are grazing, and she licks her baby dry. The mother and baby learn to recognize each other by smell and sound so that they can find each other if separated.

A calf weighs from thirty to forty pounds at birth and bears a light red or cinnamon coat instead of the dark brown one of its mother. The calf stands up within a few minutes of

being born and can run when it is just three hours old. The very young calves look much like the calves of domesticated cattle—the distinctive hump of the bison doesn't start to grow for about two months.

The calves nurse often. Bison's milk is much richer than cow's milk, but only small quantities are produced at one time. The calves also nibble at grass at an early age, but they continue to get most of their nourishment from their mothers for a long time. Bison babies are jumpy and will start at the slightest strange sound, especially when away from the mother's side. The females share in caring for the young, so that one

cow often watches over a group of calves while the other females graze. The protective cows keep the calves out of trouble, stepping between them and any possible danger.

The yearling calves, those born the year before, stay in the same herds with their mothers. Now and then a cow has been seen to let her yearling nurse even after her new calf has been born. The yearlings and two-year-olds are playful, carry-

Mothers are very protective. Here, the mother cow (left) *warns a younger cow* (right) *to stay away from her calf.*

The younger cow refuses to leave, and a fight results.

ing out brief sparring matches with their heads way down, close to the ground. A yearling will even take on a two-year-old in one of these contests. The cows and calves call to one another, creating an almost constant low rumbling sound. When a cow senses that there is anything out of the ordinary, even a mountain sheep in the path of the herd, she grunts a warning to her calf.

A typical day for bison consists of periods of grazing on a variety of grasses. These eating bouts alternate with resting times when the animals lie down and chew their cud. When they are young, the calves lie close to their mothers. While the animals graze, they move quite rapidly across the ground, taking only some of the grass as they go. Perhaps this pattern was necessary when the huge herds roamed together. It allowed animals at the rear of the group to still have plenty of food.

As spring wears on into summer, the calves begin to look more like bison. Their humps begin to grow. The tiny pair of black knobs that will become the horns develop between their ears. Their coats darken until they are the same rich brown color as their mothers. The calves spend more and more time with one another, generally in groups of five or six.

Opposite, top: *Cows rest and chew their cud, while a calf lies nearby.*

Right: *An older calf. Note the dark coat and the beginnings of the horns.*

Summer's heat brings insects that attack the bison, biting them to suck blood and laying their eggs on the animals' fur. The bison's tails flick almost constantly in an effort to keep flies away. Cowbirds perch on the buffalo's backs and feast on the insects. Bison have one other defense against the pesky flies—taking a dust bath or wallowing in the mud. The bison's habitat is marked by large patches of dusty ground that completely lack plants. The animals create these areas by raking at the ground with their horns, pulling up the plants, and by rolling in the dirt. When a bison takes a dust bath, it lowers itself slowly to the ground and then rocks back and forth on one side, raising a cloud of dust. Then it gets up and repeats the performance on the other side. The thick coating of dust that is trapped in the fur helps choke out insect pests. When it rains, the bison wallow in the resulting mud. The coating of mud dries and helps protect the skin from insects far longer than a simple dust bath.

A shaggy bison lowers itself for a dust bath. Dust flies as it bathes one side of its body and then the other.

LATE SUMMER

By late July, the bison have lost the last remnants of their winter coats. The woolly fur on the forebody contrasts strikingly with the glossy, short hair on the hind part. The hair on the bulls' heads has grown thick and dark, and their beards and pantaloons are long and heavy. The mating season, called the rut, is beginning. For the next three weeks or so, the calm routine of the herds will be interrupted by the aggressive determination of bulls in search of mates. Few bulls under the age of five will fight, even though they are able to breed by the age of four. It takes a big, strong bull to succeed in getting a mate, so a winning bull can't be too old or too young. Bulls are at their prime for breeding from ages six to ten.

A bull in late summer.

41

Most cows have their first mating when they are two years old; a few don't mate until they are three. At any given time, only some of the cows are ready to breed, so the bulls must vie for females. Spectacular battles sometimes result. At this time, several of the smaller herds of cows and calves join up to form a larger group, and the mature bulls roam about through them looking for mates. Unlike many other animals, bison bulls do

This young cow is about three years old. She has probably already borne one calf.

Tending.

not stake out areas of ground—called territories—that they defend from other males. Instead, a bull picks out one female at a time that is ready to mate and stays by her side for anywhere from a few seconds to several days.

This behavior is called tending. When a bull tends a cow, he stands closely by her side, facing the same direction, and wards off any other bulls that might come near. If the cow tries to walk off, the tending bull gets his head in front of her and keeps her from getting away.

44

The bulls interact in a variety of ways. They may bellow loudly at one another from a couple of hundred yards away, even if both are tending cows. A contending bull may stand broadside to his opponent, ten to twenty-five feet away, perhaps bellowing as he shows off his impressive size. When one bull directly challenges another, he may approach head on, stamping his feet and snorting loudly as he comes. The two animals may then approach one another closely and nod their heads up and down, starting with their heads turned slightly to the side.

Bulls avoid fighting if possible, for it takes time away from tending cows, uses up a great deal of energy, and can result in injury. A tending bull can also lose possession of a cow while he is busy fighting with another animal. Most encounters between bulls are settled by threats. One bull gives up and turns away, ending the confrontation. If a bull is backing down from a broadside threat, he may act suddenly uninterested and drop his head to graze briefly, indicating that the other bull has won that particular challenge.

The bull's tongue protrudes as he bellows a challenge to another bull.

Fights, when they do occur, can be very dramatic. The bulls face each other. One approaches the other at anything from a slow walk to a full gallop, head lowered, and bangs into his head. The thick hair on the bulls' foreheads very effectively cushions the blows. A bull that is standing still can absorb the impact of another bull at full gallop, slide back a few feet, counterattack, and win. Although the fights can sometimes go on for several minutes, they are usually over in a matter of seconds.

Another fighting strategy is called hooking. One bull cocks his head to the side and slams his forehead or horn against his opponent, often causing the other animal's front feet to come up off the ground.

The fighting can be exhausting. During the rut, lone bulls can be seen lying motionless away from the herd, exhausted or injured from the battles. Usually, serious injuries do not result from fights. But on the rare occasions when one bull attacks another from the side instead of head-on, a horn may penetrate the body and kill the animal. By the time the rut is over, the bulls have lost their sleek, neat look and may have lost as much as 300 pounds.

One bull strikes another head-on.
Next two pages: *Fast-action photos of a thirty-second battle.*

(1) Two bulls lower their heads to fight, (2) tilt them to begin a hooking attack,

(5) Heads bang. *(6) Dirt flies, and*

and (3) get so low their heads touch the ground. (4) They face off once more.

(7) *they push with all their strength.*   **(8)** *Time to attack again.*

AUTUMN

After the rut is over, the bison calm down and go back to their normal routine. The new lives will grow inside their mothers' bodies for about nine months before spring returns again and they enter the outside world. Because of the calves that were born the previous spring, the bison population is considerably larger now than it was in April, before birthing. The calves have become sturdy creatures weighing 300 to 400 pounds, and they will need plenty to eat during the winter to continue growing.

Years ago, when the bison roamed the prairie freely, they wandered over vast stretches of land, returning to the same area only after a year or more. This gave the grass that had been leveled by the buffalo plenty of time to grow back. The numbers of bison were controlled by nature—wolves and grizzly bears preyed upon the calves and old or injured animals.

But today, the bison cannot be allowed to move about at will, and their natural predators are gone. Other than some bison introduced into Alaska, the only herds not fenced in and controlled are in the Henry Mountains of Utah, Yellowstone National Park, and Wood Buffalo National Park. If food becomes scarce, the animals have no place to go to find more, and wintertime is when food is at a premium.

The bison in Custer State Park in South Dakota are fenced in and must deal with cars that travel on the road (background).

Managers at the National Bison Range look over a map of the range pastures.

Humans step in and perform the tasks formerly undertaken by nature. Important decisions must be made. How many bison can a particular area support? How many other grazing animals can safely live in any one place with them? How will the bison population be kept at a desirable level? Are there other things that should be done to maintain the herd in good health?

The National Bison Range in Moiese, Montana, which harbors a winter population of about 325 buffalo, is confined to an area of almost 19,000 acres by a tall, very sturdy fence. The fence has to be strong, for bison can plow through an ordinary pasture fence with no trouble at all. Because the range is small compared with some other places where bison live, such as Custer State Park in South Dakota, which has 73,000 acres, the animals must be especially carefully managed.

The range is divided into eight pastures by other fences, and the bison themselves are kept in two separate herds. Every three months, each herd is moved to a new pasture, so the grass in the old pasture has a chance to grow back, just as the prairie grasses once did.

The numbers of bison are kept down by rounding up the animals once a year. In August, the managers study the age and sex makeup of the herd and decide how many animals of different ages and both sexes to remove. Depending on the previous year's crop of calves, which were counted at the last roundup, from seventy to ninety animals are sold. No young calves are let go, and few animals over ten years of age are allowed to remain on the range. The managers feel that, in nature, most bison are killed by predators, fighting, or disease by the time they are ten. Because the bulls fight so intensely and sometimes die from fighting or from the weakened condition it can bring on, more cows (55 percent) are left on the range than bulls (45 percent). When these decisions have been made, a list of the animals to be selected out is published, and buyers are allowed to bid on the animals that will be available, with the bison going to the highest bidders. After the roundup, the buyers pick up their animals and take them away. Sometimes, a big bull will be purchased for a trophy head. But most

The Bison Range is located next to farmland.
A very sturdy fence (middle) *keeps the bison in.*

of the bison are used for meat, and a considerable number are bought for breeding in private herds.

The bison bred in private herds are often sold for meat, too. Buffalo meat tastes much like beef, but it is more healthful to eat. It has a third more protein than beef and 90 percent less fat. Partly because it has less fat, a bison carcass yields more meat for the producer than beef. Only about 40 percent of the bison cannot be used, while 50 percent or more of a beef carcass is wasted. In addition, buffalo heads and hides are in demand and bring good money. Bison grow well on poor pastures, and they can tolerate extremes of climate. There is a problem with raising bison, however. These big, strong animals never become completely tame and must always be treated as dangerous, wild creatures. They need lots of land to roam about, and fences must be especially strong to hold them in.

Because bison are so difficult to control, breeders have tried to cross them with cattle to produce a gentler animal that thrives on poor feed and gives tasty, lean meat. The most successful result of these attempts so far is the beefalo. Beefalo are three-eighths bison and five-eighths domestic cow. They are more efficient than cattle at turning grass into meat, and they are more adaptable to extremes in climate. Their meat is leaner than that of cattle, and they live long, productive lives.

Bison are exceptionally hardy and can withstand cold weather better than domestic cattle.

The bison roundup at Moiese takes place the first week in October. Rounding up bison is no easy task. They do not always want to go where they should. A favorite saying about these unpredictable animals is, "You can herd buffalo any place they want to go." It takes skilled, experienced cowboys riding reliable horses to get the job done.

A corridor between the two sets of pastures occupied by the two herds leads to a pasture near the roundup pens. One herd at a time is brought into this pasture. Then small groups of animals are cut from the herd—ten to twenty or so at a time —and driven down into a stout corral. The cowboys wave their hats and whoop and holler as they urge the bison down toward

the corral. They don't want the animals to have second thoughts about where they are going.

Once the bison enter the corrals, the people are in charge. The groups of bison crowd closely together, with their heads facing outward. It is very difficult to persuade one animal to leave the others.

As each animal passes through a maze of chutes, it is given a booster shot for the disease leptospirosis, and the female calves are inoculated against brucellosis. Each new calf is branded with the last digit of the current year. During the 1970s, the number was placed on the right rear side. During the 1980s, it is put on the left rear side. Because of the brand, the age of any animal on the range is easy to figure out. A few of the bison—about 7 percent—are specially marked when branded and are allowed to live out their lives on the Bison Range. These animals are weighed and evaluated each year.

Soft-drink cans tied to long poles make enough noise when rattled to help move the bison along at the roundup.

A calf is branded and given shots to protect it from developing a serious disease such as brucellosis.

Some years, other measurements are taken at the roundup. During the early 1980s, blood samples were taken from each bison. Genetic studies of the blood showed that the bison were very closely related. When one population of animals is derived from a few individuals, the genetic differences among the animals in the population can be small. Eventually, this can lead to inbreeding problems such as stillbirth or sus-

This calf was born in 1984. The 4 on its flank will make it easy to tell how old it is from now on.

ceptibility to disease. In nature, bison from different areas would mix, and any group might contain animals from different herds. On the fenced range, however, introduction of new animals must be carried out by humans. Because of the concern about inbreeding, new cows from Kansas were introduced into the National Bison Range herd in 1984. This was the first new blood in thirty-two years.

Whitetail deer fawns (above) *and a pronghorn* (below) *on the National Bison Range.*

The numbers of other large animals on the range must also be kept under control so that there is enough food for them all. Pronghorns, elk, mule deer, whitetail deer, bighorn sheep, and mountain goats also live on the bison range. Every February, about seventy volunteers come to Moiese to help count these other animals. The volunteers are divided up into groups and are taken to the top of the range to start their count. Each volunteer walks as straight a line as possible from the top to the boundary, counting every animal other than bison that he or she sees to one side. The time the animal was

Volunteers brave the cold February weather to help count other wildlife on the range.

seen and its direction of movement are also noted. At the end of the count, the records are checked over to make sure that the same animal is not counted more than once.

In the fall, the number of young animals in one group of each of these species is counted. Based on this figure and the results of the February count, the total number of animals can be estimated within about 10 percent. If some must be removed to keep them from overpopulating the range, arrangements are made for transplanting them to another area that needs more animals. Any excess deer, however, must usually be shot, since there is normally no demand in Montana for the transplanting of deer. The deer meat is given to local schools. Some years, coyotes have killed large numbers of pronghorn fawns, so the coyotes also need to be controlled to keep the pronghorn from dying out.

By the time winter arrives again, all the animals on the National Bison Range are ready. Their coats have thickened, and they will have enough to eat during the winter. Some old and sick animals will die during that harsh season, but young ones will take their place in the spring. Although humans have taken over the roles once assumed by nature, the Bison Range animals are able to live out their lives in as natural a way as possible, given the demands of civilization.

WHERE TO SEE BISON HERDS

Many zoos and private game farms have bison on exhibit. In addition, private breeders sometimes allow people to come and observe their animals. To find out about private herds in your area, or to obtain further information about bison, write to:

National Buffalo Association
P. O. Box 706
Custer, SD 57730

American Buffalo Association,
   Inc.
P. O. Box 965
Cody, WY 82414

Canadian Buffalo Association
Box 129
Earlton, Ont., Canada POJ 1EP0

The following state and national parks have buffalo herds that can be viewed by visitors:

CANADA

Banff National Park
Alberta

Elk Island National Park
Alberta

Prince Albert National Park
Saskatchewan

Riding Mountain National Park
Manitoba

Waterton Lakes National Park
Alberta

Wood Buffalo National Park
Alberta/NW Terr.

COLORADO
Colorado National Monument
Fruita

ILLINOIS
Fort Massac State Park
Metropolis

KANSAS

Maxwell Game Refuge
Canton

Crawford County State Lake
Pittsburg

KENTUCKY

State Game Farm
Frankfort

MINNESOTA

Blue Mounds State Park
Luverne

MONTANA

National Bison Range
Moiese

NEBRASKA

Fort Niobrara National Wildlife
Refuge
Valentine

NORTH CAROLINA

Pisgah National Forest and Game
Preserve

NORTH DAKOTA

Sully's Hill National Game
Refuge
Fort Totten

Theodore Roosevelt National
Memorial Park
Medora

OKLAHOMA

Witchita Mountain National
Wildlife Refuge
Cache

Platt National Park
Sulphur

SOUTH DAKOTA

Custer State Park
Hermosa

Wind Cave National Park
Hot Springs

Badlands National Monument
Interior

TEXAS

LBJ State Park
Stonewall

WYOMING

Grand Teton National Park
Moose

Hot Springs State Park
Thermopolis

Yellowstone National Park

INDEX

Page numbers in *italics* refer to captions.